POETRY now

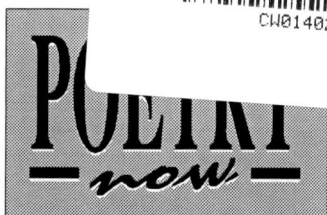

THE HILLS ARE ALIVE

Edited by

Chiara Cervasio

First published in Great Britain in 2004 by
POETRY NOW
Remus House,
Coltsfoot Drive,
Peterborough, PE2 9JX
Telephone (01733) 898101
Fax (01733) 313524

SB ISBN 1 84460 770 4

FOREWORD

Although we are a nation of poets we are accused of not reading poetry, or buying poetry books. After many years of listening to the incessant gripes of poetry publishers, I can only assume that the books they publish, in general, are books that most people do not want to read.

Poetry should not be obscure, introverted, and as cryptic as a crossword puzzle: it is the poet's duty to reach out and embrace the world.

The world owes the poet nothing and we should not be expected to dig and delve into a rambling discourse searching for some inner meaning.

The reason we write poetry (and almost all of us do) is because we want to communicate: an ideal; an idea; or a specific feeling. Poetry is as essential in communication, as a letter; a radio; a telephone, and the main criterion for selecting the poems in this anthology is very simple: they communicate.

CONTENTS

THE FOUR SEASONS

Spring warms the earth
Bringing plants to life once more
Birds building their nests
To rear their young
Summer brings sunshine and warmth
Gardens a riot of colour
From numerous plants
Filling the air with sweet perfume
Daffodils stand proud
A mass of gold
Autumn brings cooler days
Trees blowing in the wind
Leaves turning from green to gold
To take a rest, for another year
Winter draws near
With cold winds and snow
Freezing the earth
In its icy grip
Woodlands transformed
Into a winter wonderland
The cycles complete
For another year.

Alice Higham

TEACH ME

Teach me to dance with shimmering wings
And glory in the sun
To skip around the scented flowers
Till happy days are done.

Teach me to walk with uplift face
And revel in the rain
To feel the wind upon my face
And count the day as gain.

Teach me to walk through rustling leaves
And crunch through virgin snow
In simple pleasures to rejoice
And joy through seasons know.

Wesley Stephens

JOURNEY HOME

Beached on cold shingle,
a little grey seal
Sad and bedraggled
Great eyes gazing at a
frightening world
Sick little orphan
lost and forlorn, curled
on the shingle . . .

And comes to him
a human brother
who carries him, tender
as lost mother,
to sanctuary
To tend and nurture and heal
the lost little seal,
to fulfil his destiny . . .

Home to the sea,
strong now and free
Back to the wild
the little grey seal orphan child . . .

And his guardian angel smiled.

Jo Lee

A PLACE UNSPOILED

We breathed the air so pure that day
As we observed the scene before us -
High above the River Tarn
We watched it wind and turn
Exposing yellowed banks
Hot from the summer sun.

Vultures soaring with wings outstretched
Circling, swooping as they searched for prey,
Commanding the towering cliffs
We felt small below their path
But shared the same pure air
Hot from the summer sun.

High-walled corridors of rock
Sheltered the beauty of the gorge,
Medieval villages clung to cliffs
Sculptured to the rocky faces
We observed this hidden place
Hot in the summer sun.

Mair Walters

A CHARTWELL DAY

There was the shiny blue lake
Half hidden between rolling green lawns
Backed by trees not yet in full bloom
So when the bluebells come soon . . .
This is an encouragement to dream
To honour the memory of times past
A quiet abode, water lilies
Decorating a tiny lake
Where future life was cast.
A small spring of running water, the many
Shrubs hiding in dark undergrowth
Entwined with flowers of every hue.
One can almost hear the distant sounds
Of war, planned here, long
Since gone, but the echoes stay.
A place of quiet beauty
Where the crowds come to respect
This noble homestead, where all the echoes,
Thoughts and feelings are never swept away.

Joan Hands

THE BLUEBELL WOOD

Yes, I remember the bluebell wood
Slivers of sunlight darting down
From tall tree tops into cool shadow
And sheltered greenness.

A floor of flowers, delicate blues
From the softness of summer skies
Fragile stalks trembling upwards
From earth's darkness.

Far from school or office
From that stifling proliferation of paper
The wood breathed its primal magic
Without word, without sound.

An Eden of a thousand bluebells
And no one to measure or count
Show on screens, file statistics
Compare and contrast or even
Pick to die in pretty vases.

Just a wild sea of blue
And the silent music
Of wind-caressed bells
Calling the trees to prayer
And to the wood's evensong.

Chris Woodland

AUTUMN SURPRISES

Autumn tints hovering near
Leaves green still a few
Beauty fading of summer scenes
Change of seasons welcomed anew.

Beauty of buds' past growth
Shades of forest green
Zest new giving to spirit, soul
Pleasure for all to see, feel.

Purple shades of night
Charm of woodland trees
Song birds, feathers bright
Music from nestlings on leafy canopies.

Landscape colourful nigh
Blessing of sunset, sunrise
Change of seasons to abide
Glory from above, to surprise, surprise.

Ivy Lott

DAY'S END

Evening tints in the western sky;
nebulous beams stretching across space,
streaking the heavens with warmth:
prophet of the morrow's splendour.

The gilded ripples yield
to a bronze and copper swell:
a sea of crimson waves breaks
upon the cerulean firmament.

Ever changing skyscape -
fanfaring the end of another day.
The transitory sunset
dissolves
into night.

Joy Morton

BIRTH OF SPRING

Snowdrops, like bright stars,
Signal the end of winter's gloom,
A carpet of crocus appears . . .
Like a rainbow,
Then the daffodils bloom.

They herald the birth of spring,
You can almost hear their tune,
A fanfare parade . . . as a
Troop of buglers at dawn.

The primrose arrives quietly,
Softly lighting the coppice floor,
Spring flowers . . . nature's delight,
Winter is with us no more.

William Moyle Breton

A DROWNING NATION

It is a sprinkling of atolls
lost in the South Pacific
it looks like paradise
with its lush vegetation
and its Gauguinesque hues
but here they dream of Venice
not because of the fabled beauty
of the City of the Doges
but because it has been sinking
for the last two or three centuries
you would think them cynical
not at all, for they know
the world is trying to rescue it
whereas in their islands
there is no such hope
the warming of our planet
has got the better of them
and a cyclone can wipe
those atolls from the face
of the Earth in one sweep
this could happen next week
in a month, with luck, in a year
the government has started
to evacuate the people of Tuvalu
and have asked
Australia and New Zealand
to grant them asylum
but the two island nations
counter the fact that the
disaster hasn't occurred yet
and that they cannot consider
the people of Tuvalu
as environmental refugees

there are eleven thousand of them
eleven thousand citizens
who will soon speak of their
country in the past.

Albert Russo

AUGUST

I lay gently dozing on a hillside
on a warm, bright, summer's day.
I could hear a distant combine
cutting the last of the hay.
The fleeting form of a bird
flashes across my vision
and the scurrying feet of a creature
fades into oblivion.
A soft caress of a breeze
soothes my warming skin
and dances across my body
calming the soul within.
The tantalising smell of the grass,
the flowers and the trees,
the whispered rustling insects
join hypnotic droning bees.
A wisp of hair tickles my face,
and I raise my hand dreamily
to put it back in place.
It's then I decide, the countryside
must be just like Heaven.

Jaimee P Nix

AUTUMN SOLSTICE

Blue tits visit Elder tree
Her branches fully laden
Bramble fruit for all to see
A banquet for a maiden
Hawthorn berries, darkest red
Alongside wild roses
All give healing it is said
As well as pretty posies
Next to ripen, Apple bough
With fruit to heal the sick
Come gather up her bounty now
Or choose a lucky stick
'Neath Hazel stand with open hand
To catch a tasty nut
This wise man of the wood
Will open eyes which have been shut
Amid all these, our sacred trees
The Oak will be the grandest
He lives at length to give us strength
Just as nature planned it
Great Mother Beech is here to teach
And give us welcome shelter
She rustles as you pass beneath
I'm sure that you have felt her
From woodland now to open field
Fetch corn, oats and barley
A time for harvesting their yield
For folk who know the country
Let's give thanks for autumn then
With all the gifts she brings
This joyful time for food and wine
While happy bird life sings.

Deborah Hall

BE

I often ponder trivial things
Does grass mean itself to grow
To provoke pleasure? And do flowers know
How much they mean to beloved or lover?
And why the beauty, and why it looks just so.

I love pretending oaks demand to hold themselves so high,
To reach for some creator, and on the way caress the sky.
Do the mountains really yearn to one another,
Rolling just to let their fingers meet? I reconsider;

In this place, absorbed by silence -
Rare and precious freedom of the mind;
My thoughts absolved from judge and jury,
Those damning eyes of humankind.

I don't think I've ever given
Such intent consideration,
To realise actions can hold no reason
And some things just merely live and 'be',

Mankind, I see, does like to think
All living things should also strive
To find cause and reason in being alive
Just as fervently as he.

It seems now, such a wretched crime
To attribute passion upon this innocent stem,
Who knows not that it's growing,
Nor fight the breeze that without knowing
Makes the blade to bend.

Georgina Milne (17)

REST A WHILE

Do you want to rest a while
And look upon this lake so still?
Would you like to comfort me
And play the merry song?

Look upon the trees and flowers
Growing in shapes of none that we see
Look upon birds and insects small
And sun and moon does go within.

And in the house of silk and lace
A quietness remains
Memories of buns and lemons
Create a crystal haze.

Reflections of a life so calm
A dragonfly goes by
Stirring thoughts and dreams alike
This place is life's recall.

Juliana Moon

SUNFLOWER

Face raised in prayer,
the sunflower worships the sun
until darkness falls.

Like a disciple,
it follows the Master's steps
in adoration

shadowing His path
like a parched acolyte or
dipsomaniac;

a golden trumpet,
proclaiming the love of God,
until it shrivels.

This great sunflower
from Provence, embracing us
like a universe.

Norman Bissett

IN THE INTERIM

Still the leaves are of emerald hue,
with leaves in profusion, the fall yet to come,
and the breeze, unwavering,
chasing the flouncing clouds
across a chilled blue sky.
The sea, down from the hill,
bears waves that dance, roll and jump
in silver-flecked joy over its depth.
Soon, the wind, rain and snow will return,
but today the sun belies the season.
I gaze in wonder, marvelling
at this glorious day,
in the interim.

Jennifer Richards

ETERNAL SPRING

Autumn colours blaze
In splendid loveliness
Around me.

Seasons mingle in my head,
Leaves turn catkin yellow,
Tulip red,
And float like cherry blossom
Down to mellow earth
Confusing me.

Mists weave their way
Like early morning dew
In springtime.
Golden tendrils drape
From shrubbery and vine,
Bewitching me.

My body and my soul
Burst forth in buds anew,
Enticingly.
I will not bow to seasons,
Conform to expectations
Constricting me.

No autumn in my life,
But sweet and beautiful
Eternal spring.

Sue Percival

BUDS ARISING FROM THE SUBJECT OF BUDS

Come, gentle spring, ethereal mildness, come,
And, from the bosom of yon dropping cloud,
While music wakes around, veiled a shower . . .
Of shadowing roses, on our plains descend.
O rainbow garden, fitted or to shine in courts
With unaffected grace, or walk the plain,
With innocence and mediation joined . . .
In soft assemblage, listen to my song, many colours . . .
Seven colours of the rainbow, it's so bright there,
Which they own season paints; when nature all is here,
Is blooming and benevolent, like thee.
And see where surely winter passes off, into the sunset . . .
Far to the north, and calls his ruffian blasts.
His blasts obey, and quit the howling hills, of wonder colours,
The shattered forest and the ravaged value; hot stuff . . .
While softer gales succeed, at whose kind touch, many colours,
The mountains lift their green heads to the sky.
As yet the trembling year is unconfirmed in any day,
And winter oft at eve resumes the breeze, within all colours . . .
Chills the gale morn, and bids his driving sleets . . .
Deform the day delightless; so that scares . . .
The bittern knows his time, with bill engulfed
To shake the sounding marsh; or, from the shore,
The plovers when to scatter o'er the heath,
And sing their wild notes to the listening waste.
Ye softening dews, ye tender showers descend!
Have done their part. Ye fastening breezes, blow!
And temper all plants, thou world-reviving sun, new rainbow . . .
Into the perfect year! Nor ye who live, in the full height.

Viv Lionel Borer

OLD WOODLAND TRACK

Where scented flowers in spring grow,
After the last of the winter snow.
Fragrances fill the spring air,
And plenty of it for all to share.

Foxgloves, bluebells, nod their tiny bells,
Seems to break the magic spells.
Baby rabbits come out to play,
When it is a beautiful day.

As the rippling waters flow,
Lively wildlife starts to show.
New leaves rustle in the breeze,
Blowing blossoms from the trees.

Often I go through the wood,
The old tree has gone where I often stood,
But the memories will come back,
As I follow the old woodland track.

Margaret Upson

LATE AUTUMN

A shadow galleon ghosts
the cold, clear, crystal sky
where a diamond solitaire sparkles.
As gold shimmers the silver birch,
and rosehips gleam in October's
warm sun beams,
a robin flashes his bright breast,
his eyes twinkling . . .

Anita Richards

DOWN AT STURMINSTER NEWTON MILL

Along the slow, swirling river
The old mill stands.
Always tossing upwards,
Hurrying as fast as it can!
Just past a great noisy wheel
Is a rolling scene.
A row of faint willows
Hold their whispering keenly.
Further down the stream is so still
And the lovely lilies
Are white and real.
The wild bee dozes
And the thought of being stung
Would bring aggravation -
And not of roses!
The drowsiness of the sweet meadow alluring stands,
A gathering of honeysuckle
Stretches out its inviting hands.
Where beauty of nature supremely uncloses
Is to give thanks to God for the comforts
And everlasting joy it reposes.

Sammy Michael Davis

A WINTER AFTERNOON

The pale gold sun,
clouds of white silk,
clouds of dove grey,
a winter afternoon.

An angel in a cloud,
in attitude of western prayer
or eastern greeting,
combines the two.

A winter afternoon,
evening comes so soon.

The clouds turn pink and lilac,
the sun blushes
to a blazing fire.

Jacqueline Ives

FEEDING THE WILDLIFE

On my way to the shops yesterday,
I passed two little grey squirrels bobbing along.
It's hard to say who was more surprised.
I watched them scurry up the tree before my eyes.
Last night I looked out of the window
And what did I see? A little red fox, running across the street.
Was she looking for food or shelter?
Why is man's desire to destroy nature so strong,
That he is leaving no place for the wildlife to go but the city?
I threw bread out for the birds; it was only a sparrow who came,
But now I see the crows, magpies and seagulls too.
The poor little sparrow is last in the queue.
And now the little robin has joined in the fight.
Maybe one day man will get it right
And leave somewhere for the animals so they won't take flight.
No wonder they call her Mother Nature.

Christie Forfar

UMBRELLAS OF PROVENCE

Those dark undulations are monsters
that you see on your way through Provence,
cast into mountains by ancient spells
they guide your path to the Côte.

Mottling green shadows on their backs
are macqui and umbrella pine,
while lines of patterned plane trees
strobe perspectives of sun-drenched roads.

But along the ways of the Côte d'Azure
the umbrellas reign supreme;
in darkened clusters or solitary state,
in rapport they live with man.

Arranged in tiers on hillsides
summer homes squat facing the sea;
green spreads of caring umbrellas
spin away the rampant Mistral.

In straight or contorted posture
they characterise those shores,
and wave across the Tropezian Gulf
to their kin on the rounding coast.

Bougainvillaea spill lustrous purples
on ubiquitous, sandstone walls
and with shrubs of bright lantana
share the colour prize of the Côte.

But, alone, the umbrellas the late stage hold,
darkly sketched along the strand
against a tonal sky-wash,
gently brushed by departing sun.

Ron Hails

NATURE

When all around is confusion
And noise
Nature quietly, gently, employs
Its perfect plan for its perfect
World, and all its beauty is unfurled.
And while we struggle, and scream
And shout,
Nature quietly goes about
Building again, what man
Has destroyed,
With unending patience,
To fill the void.

W J Doyle

NATURE

Nature in the raw
With power beyond compare
Which bursts forth from the womb
Of Mother Earth, so rare.

The birth of molten lava
Spewed in temper hot
To run amok
Where'er it will.

To cover and bury
All that stands its ground
Leaving desolation
For times' immortal view.

No more growth
The crop of green has gone
To leave the black
Misshapen idle waste.

A V R Cracknell

HIBERNATION

Onset of winter
Cold black skies
Frosty mornings

Trudging in snow
Digging out cars
Clearing paths

Pass the salt

Loss of power
National gridless
No heat, no television

Snuggle-in-bed season
Reluctant to rise
Hibernation is the answer.

Dawn Sansum

MELLOW OCTOBER

Webs of lace shimmering
On dawn's frosty hedgerows,
Sap flowing down to roots,
Like mercury in a barometer,
In trees performing strip-tease,
Shedding leaves burnt to a crisp.

Miniature haystacks
Of garden refuse on fire,
Emitting acrid smoke,
Catching throats, stinging eyes,
While sleepy hedgehogs
Quick-step their way
From within the bonfires' hearts,
With smouldering feet
And smoking spines,
Snuffling indignantly
At nearly being baked alive.

Before twilight spreads its protective cloak,
An expanding bloodshot sun,
Turns lake and ponds crimson.
Nature now ready for slumber,
Brings a touch of sadness,
Redeemed only by wistful thoughts
Of next year's spring.

Raymond W Seaton

STILL WATER

The tide is high
As the swans glide by
On liquid glass,
Like clouds
Drifting across
A cold, green sky.

Purple flowers swim
At the water's edge,
Where earth
And river merge
In silent tranquillity.

Long fingers of willow
Trail lightly
Over the shining surface,
And I long to keep
This moment of complete peace
Locked forever in my heart.

Mary Ellis

SPRING GLORY

The beat of nature's heart is set in motion
As the first breath of spring is cast
Perfect clouds waft across a clear blue sky
From beneath a blanket of frost
Emerging buds a sure sign of spring
Plants waking from their winter slumber.
Evenings lengthen, growing lighter
Animals prepare for their offspring's birth.
Warm breezes blow the sweet scent of blossom.
Never-ending birdsong whistling in the trees.
Steams flow on their way to the sea.
Spring cleaning, it has to be done,
Washing lines full, laundry blowing.
Snowdrops, tulips are in full bloom.
Nature has opened its eyes to a brand new day,
Spreading warmth and sunlight across the land.
Spring is showing its true glory.

Jo Lodge

RAW SPIRIT, QUICKLY

Bells tolling in the distance
Sweet, sweet birds, things more
Than that mere name – melodious
Bright yet mild and living, singing!
Rolling fields of perfection, green and
Wet with water of the mid
Sky and earth - green and possessing
More than simple earth - earth, what
A vital name . . . the sky, wet yet again,
Water everywhere - speech in the sky
Blue so blue and then infused with a
Paler character in autumn and winter . . .
Perfect autumn, perfect autumn . . .

Thomas Conor

AN AUTUMN JOG

Crisp autumn air
Cool pale sun
Wet gleaming pavements
Dewy grass

Ploughed brown furrows
White frosty ridges
Spindly trees
Black and stark

Farmyard aromas
Friendly bellows
Snorts and grunts
New-mown hay

Barking dogs
Piercing whistle
Distant voices
Float away.

Geraldine Taylor

THE LAKE

I savoured music's sweet, mesmeric moods
well in advance of its advent,
imagination rife in interludes
when hushed daydreaming time was spent;
plagues of the day were interspersed with tone,
lingering like essential light,
the life-blood of my soul I bore alone,
its tedium, its terror, blight;
then wait, protracted, reaped desired award
though somewhere still, as yet inept,
Heaven held its notes, then I gazed toward
a scene I'd watched when once I slept,
a rainbow view of roses' mute appeal,
medley of miracles, they too
were beautiful as bars, they made me feel
inspired, I wondered, 'Is this true?'
A Gulliver, ungainly was my tread,
sojourner from the planet Earth,
and Lilliputian lovelies, pink and red,
below me, tokens of re-birth.
I faintly thought, 'What peace shall Mozart make?
Can this serenity exist
and more?' And then, through trees, I glimpsed the lake,
climactic coda that I missed
before, the ultimate in perfect rest,
it lay, all sound, all shade made manifest.

Ruth Daviat

MY AUTUMN GARDEN

Hot, fiery oranges, pink pastels of every shade,
Lemon and the lilacs, cerise and purple haze,
Gold and scarlet leaves soon will drop and swiftly fade,
White blooms entwine with copper bushes,
Tinged with a golden glow,
Soon all will be lost,
Beneath soft, pearlised snow.

In warm rays of October all clings with dew of morning.
Many flowers are caught in Mrs Spider's spell,
Gossamer garlands woven, for each their adorning
From each leaf hang sparkling gems,
Rainbow droplets in the sun's smile,
Slowly trickling down velvet stems.

Willows are rustling their crinoline gowns,
Paint box leaves float away on the breeze,
Gradually the lawn will be a patchwork eiderdown,
My garden is quite a magical place,
An oasis of colour
In nature's seasons of taste.

Susan E Roffey

THE DARKEST DAY

The gentle tingling suddenly changes to sharp stinging pain
Raining down on my face and head
The feeling of being stabbed by a million tiny needles all at once
Clothes being torn from my body as I struggle wildly
Against an unseen force
All around me darkness looms enveloping me in its
Cold forbidding womb
Suddenly a flash of brilliant white light pierces my eyes
But before I can capture vision
The sound of a thousand bull elephants stampeding the
Arid plains of Africa in their search for cooling water
Invading my ears and roaring through my brain
Fear grips like steel bands so my heart thumps madly in my chest
Like the fierce beating of a tom-tom
Legs heavy as iron girders, breath heaving, rasping
Catching in my throat as I run
Desperately trying to escape this terrifying storm.

Madeleine R Searle

VIEW FROM THE WINDOW

Placid with cattle
fields slide gently down,
where broadleaves' vowels
write their rounded way
along a stream's winding.
Dippers tread its rushing pebble floor,
dragonflies' blue flames lick the surface.

A narrow lane scales
facing valley sides
snowed up with clover.
Industrious bees
echo tractors, ploughing
middle distance till conifers' sharp
consonants rise to pink the skyline.

Buzzard's silent sword
quarters his self-mapped
world of emptiness,
measured in wing beats,
glides and whorls on upward
thermals. Young, mewing, learn on summer
winds this aerial cartography.

Elinor Wilson

THE FOREST AT NIGHT

The forest at night is a mysterious place
The sounds that you hear magnetize in the dark
Those rustling sounds, so menacing it seems,
Is just a mouse scurrying home.
The beautiful sound of the nightingale song
Is a bonus you cannot beat.
The hoot of the owl as he hunts for his prey
The sudden rush of sounds as down he swoops
And the squeal of the victim,
As he bears it away to his nest high in the trees.
The silvery gleam as the moon reaches its height,
Makes shadows as long as the eye can see.
The starlight is bright on this frosty night
As it glistens on cobwebs the spiders have spun,
Waiting to trap when daybreak comes
Any unsuspecting insect as they fly by.
As the first threads of light appear in the sky
The forest at night begins to awake
With its dawn chorus away on the wing,
As another night is over and a new day begins.

Patricia Turner

THE WHITE ROSE

One night I saw myself out my window
I was standing staring up toward the dark sky
I looked hopeful yet I felt sad.
I slowly turned my head down
and saw a tear roll down my face.
It paused on my chin
and then slowly dropped towards the ground.
It seemed to fall forever
and finally smashed open upon the floor
and out of the tear stretched a white rose.
It grew up toward the night
and then quietly opened into a beautiful
array of lines and swirling circles.
I saw myself reach out for it
and as my hand moved forward
the flower began to fall.
I tried to call out
but I couldn't.
The flower fell and withered into the soil
and onto the place where it lay; dropped another silver tear.

Mark Stead

Autumn Glory

A simple leaf falling
Climate on the change
Gold and bronzes - a pure delight
Swirling graciously to the ground
A natural carpet appears
Autumnal glory all around
A chill in the air
Hibernation is calling
Survival is the key
Camouflage and warmth
Nature's blanket for one and all
Magical, mysterious autumn is here.

Anne Sackey

NATURE

Metallic,
The light
On those
Trees,
Birch,
By the roadside,
A touch of France?
Leaves turn to
Plum, aubergine
Dance,
Summer is over,
No need to
Grieve.

Janet M Baird

THE RIVER

Lovely the river's rushing flow
The chromatic breaking of tumbling water
Spiritually ghost-like
As if from Medusa's dark blood
Pegasus is rising misty
As fine-spun angel's hair.

Louise Mills

A SAPPHIRE AND EMERALD SPHERE

I am but one speck,
Set in an ocean of indescribable beauty,
Cast adrift into infinite possibilities,
Whereon life in its endless forms,
Could seize reality,
And inhabit the multi landscapes,
On this surface of my sphere,
Planet Earth,

At conception I experienced the light source,
And was but an element,
That integrated joining with atoms and gases,
As we filled the void,
I participated in the dance of life,
Witnessed form in its many guises,
The intertwining of dark and light,
Merging and forming the celestial heavens,

Eons passed expanding into that named the universe,
Then I became woven into the planet Earth,
I am at its heartbeat
And in its very breath,
The energy source,
Wrought life in all its forms,
From the microscopic to the gigantean,
All sought the haven that was terra,

Extinction wrought its hand for certain species,
A game of chance, survival of the fittest,
Eventually the life form known as Homo-Sapiens,
Inhabited the lush and verdant landscape,
And were to be Earth's guardians,
In this age, some seek to destroy the natural world,
Earth mother, ancient name Gaia,
This the sapphire and emerald sphere.

Ann G Wallace

THE RAINBOW

Raindrops falling like teardrops from the arc of the rainbow.
Seeming to touch the chapel tower as people wander towards it
Reaching up their arms, at last to find the rainbow's end?
Disappointment on faces as they feel nothing.
Where gone that pot of gold they say is at the rainbow's end?
A child sitting on a nearby gravestone sees a gleam of gold,
She reaches out to grab it and finds in her small hands
A fluttering yellow butterfly.
She lets it go, as it soars away the people look up.
The rain now pouring onto upturned faced.

Marj Busby

OCTOBER MOON

I watched it grow night by night -
No, in fact, that's not quite right,
For some nights were cloud-cloaked
And some I didn't look,
But it grew, all the same,
Four weeks, by the book.

It grew from a thin sickle,
Polished like an old nickel.
It grew to half-size, shaped
Like a country cheese.
It grew larger, then
Came the midnight breeze.

Tossing in a sleepless state,
I pulled the curtains back, 'Oh wait!
There hangs a lantern cream
With mystical figure,
Glorious and majestic,
Brighter still and bigger.'

Each month gives us this wonder -
The sight of silent thunder;
But October reigns supreme,
Dark, baleful clouds scud past
Thrust by the autumn gales.
The moon triumphs at last.

No wonder ancient people worshipped the moon,
Autumn is past and winter comes, all too soon.

D M Anderson

IGUANAS IN THE EVENING AT UXMAL

The history of the ancients stands silhouetted against the fading light,
As evening exacts its toll upon the day,
And myriad cicadas serenade the setting sun,
In a scene of ever-changing visual and auditory cacophony.
The colours of the world fade from pastel to dark,
And the great pyramid of the ancients commands awe in the eye
of the beholder.

I sat upon the weathered steps once trod by long-dead priests and rulers,
Steps saturated by the day-long heat of the once revered and
worshipped sun.
Rising from the jungle, reaching out to touch the sky,
The stones bear witness to the passage of the past.
The Maya are no longer, their history obscure,
But El Pyramide del Adivino is as real as I.

I close my eyes, and in the gathering gloom
I can almost hear the sound of warriors in joyful song,
Of people's voices raised in celebration, when this was a city of life.
But no, this is just my mind at play, and there, at the causeway's end,
Rafael Montoya leads his weary mule home for the night,
Another day of selling souvenirs to the tourists at an end.

A sudden rush of sound above my head, I look up and there I see,
A flock of yellow warblers, so many they fill the sky, as they head
towards their roosting trees.
The shadows of the past lengthen, night will soon be here,
But I am transfixed by my own reverie, as I sit upon the ancient steps.
As the stones grow cooler, and the sun sinks lower, I sense more
than see
Movement all around me, and the steps and stones become alive.

Iguanas, large and small, converge upon the temple,
And, ignoring me in their single-mindedness, they bypass me without
a thought.
I watch, transfixed, as every crack and every niche in every stone
is occupied.
And I think that maybe the pyramid is still a place of worship, of a kind.
Sun-worshippers, cold-blooded, in need of the life-sustaining warmth of
the mighty sun,
And where better to retreat when the cool of night invades their
reptilian world?

The steps and stones on which I sit hold the warmth of the passing sun,
For an iguana in search of a bed, a centrally-heated citadel.
I lose count of their numbers, but watch until the parade is done,
I begin to descend, but as I go, I turn, look back, see a straggler wriggle
into a vacant crack.
And as the Pyramid of the Magician stands in silhouette against
the moonlight,
I walk slowly home, and my dreams that night are filled with ancient
warriors and sleeping iguanas . . .

Juan Pablo Jalisco

OVER THE HILLS AND FAR AWAY

We dream and dream of life that's far away.
Over the hills and out of sight.
There could be flowers and unknown place to stray,
Could there be grass to play our games?
Would there be peace
And friendships too?

Could there be people from other planets and worlds?
Might I meet my man again?
But then he might be different my inside curled.
We might have grown apart by now,
I would have aged,
Not he!

Over the hills and far away, new life,
Maybe, perhaps, old life, who knows?
Coal for heating, gas for light, what strife,
No televisions, few cars, no national health,
Despair, depression,
Unless very rich!

Over the hills and far away as ghosts,
Maybe, but hopefully not with the devil.
Perhaps enjoy a holy life, foremost?
Must be peaceful, stop meandering!
Life will
Go on!

B Mills

GOD'S ARTWORK

We may appreciate works of art;
but God's artwork is the best.
I love the warm, shining sun,
streaming through my window.
It seems to beckon and encourage,
the sky a dusky blue, with clouds like cotton wool.
The trees swaying in the breeze,
changing with the seasons; interesting.
I love going out for walks, past houses and trees,
where the wonder of nature springs back at me.
It's lovely to see people's vibrant,
coloured gardens, decked with flowers.
Although their love and care has gone in to it,
God made it all possible;
so to Him we praise and worship.
He seems to be saying, 'Peace with you.'
In this troubled world, nature and flowers
can minister to us;
reminding us that there is beauty to be found,
and a joy and peace in nature.
The birds fly freely about, seeming without care.
We, too, can feel free and at one with nature.
And when winter passes and spring begins,
we can rejoice when the cycle renews.
We too will be renewed, if we let it be,
for God is always working in all that He made.
Such a wonder is His artwork, made for us to enjoy.

Christina Gilbert

A Moment's Reflection In Autumn

It's only a leaf.
Red-gold, crumpled, blown by the breeze,
One of a hundred, a thousand,
Which swirl in the crisp air, whirl, fall, dance,
Heralding the cold of the coming winter.

It's only a leaf.
Child of the parent tree it robed in glory,
One of a hundred, a thousand,
Which fashioned green shelter,
Gave cool shade, freely, in the heat of the summer.

It's only a leaf.
It will be muddied, blackened, kicked aside, trod underfoot.
One of a hundred, a thousand,
I hold it in my hand, smooth it, reflect a moment, wonder,
It's only a leaf, dying, but it's beautiful.

June Holmes

ON A SUMMER BREEZE

Thistle seeds and dandelion clocks,
Dance with the summer breeze,
While butterflies flitter,
Amongst flowers with ease,
Tall and majestic,
Pink and blue,
Or small and delicate,
White or a different hue.
Buzzards soar,
In a blue, blue sky,
While cotton wool clouds,
Sail by,
Fields of corn,
Grow more than waist high,
And where no man can see them,
Baby animals hide,
When the summer sun shines,
And summer scents flow by,
Windows open,
And the green trees sigh,
Night-time brings stars,
Twinkling bright,
And a moon,
That lights up the night.

Hannah Freeman

LATE OCTOBER IN CHURNET VALLEY

Enchanting Churnet valley,
Its hillsides swathed in trees,
Each leaf and bough dripping
In the aftermath of last night's rain.
Within this narrow, water-fed valley,
The river is turbulent, fast flowing,
On its headlong rush to the River Trent,
And the far distant North Sea.
The ground abounds in mounds
Of bright, newly fallen leaves.
Great bonfire heaps of colours,
From pure gold, lemon and tawny,
To ones still green, or orange and ruby.
Slippy, in the first stages of decay,
Yet spice-scented as an Arabian bazaar.
Riverlets of water cascade down the hills,
Gravity-driven to find the fast flowing river.
A dank, rising wind makes me shiver,
As a million more leaves tumble down.
This ancient place seems set in aspic.
Quaint centuries old cottages abound,
Like treasured memories from times long gone.
Tiny gardens still pretty with autumn flowers,
Victorian dahlias and a star-blaze of Michaelmas daisies
And the gold, red and russet, of fall chrysanthemums.
It appears some ancient Norse god once walked here,
And with me today, this fierce being walks still.
I sigh contentedly, measuring moments, steadily walking.
Churnet valley, caught in magic, beautiful beyond words.

Jonathan Pegg

SEASONS' BEAUTY

The beauty of our world is in the seasons' change,
Autumn is here.
With glorious colours in the fading leaves,
Fulfilment in the air.

The hills, the fields and woods are
Going to their rest in winter cold.
Before they go, they shine in softer glow
Of brown and gold.

Then winter with its frosty patterns
Takes its place with cold north wind,
To freeze the lake and silver every tree
With hoary rind.

But spring returns and all the land awakes
From winter sleep.
The grass and trees are green again upon the hills
And streams run deep.

Flowers, birds and butterflies awaken too,
And birds will sing.
All the lovely landscape will rejoice
In time of spring.

The long hot days of summer will soon follow on,
With cloudless skies,
More glorious colours cover gardens, hedgerow, woods
Where summer lies.

And so, the cycle of the changing year
Will give us joy.
We can drink in the gladness of all nature's gifts;
Here to enjoy.

Mary Johnson-Riley

RIDING THE MARCHES (A TANKA)

Suffolk's summer glow,
Barbed briar blossoming around
Chameleon corn,
Blue flax now where mad hares ran,
Changeless change all about me.

Peter Davies

LAKE MORNING

Morning light
freshens the lake,
white feather crisp:
deserting swans lift -
wings beating,
life, life, life.

Watch the wind,
thistle thick,
in aimless patterns
blow a skin of lilac
where once ochred paths
wait dust shaded.

Sun-smiling air breathes
through dry-reeded
shivering day.
I hunt this happiness
ravenous, examining each leaf's
vivid celebration.

Fay Emerson

THE BUZZARD

My attention is drawn by your plaintive cry,
Then I see you soaring way up high.
On the thermals of air you glide around,
While all the time you're watching the ground.
A sudden swoop onto prey unsuspecting,
Your presence it's a little late detecting.
Up you rise to your feeding perch,
Sate your hunger, then resume your search.
I watch you with your wings spread wide,
While all the little creatures run and hide.
Your aerial displays are spectacular indeed,
Circling gently, then a dive at speed.
You hover so still, completely suspended,
You are what you are, as nature intended.
So beautiful buzzard with your beady eye,
Continue to soar with your plaintive cry,
For I love to watch your incredible display,
As on the thermals you hunt and play.

Ruth Robinson

SUMMER

Walking the riverbank
Just for the sound.

Then:
Sitting on a rock,

Bending,
Letting cold water
Push against the palm,

Fingers feeling pebbles
Scrape.

Bare feet. Cold water,
Watching a brown trout
Jumping, lazy ripples spreading.

Thinking.

Breathing.

Billy Campbell

THE CHERRY TREE

When spring rushed past my hopeful door
rustling your tiny leaves
you brought me enchanting hopes,
adorned with wiry arms with yarns of cherry blossoms
lighting my face, I smiled.

When summer came with a fragranced breath
I threw my dreams in the air carelessly,
you gave me a haven of petals weaving spells, I yearned.

I watched my dreams changing shapes
moving beyond the milky way reaching for joy.
You stood silently watching my star sign
speeding across the night sky weeping instead.
I moved, leaving you holding the earthern roots of life.

When autumn comes to my garden
it will free your thoughts again.
When harvest moon shines like a sleepy secret
it will soothe you again.
While northern wind knocked on my door calling,
I scribbled on a matchbox a memoir to the cherry tree.
You were a delightful chapter of my passing youth.

Tanuja Kumari Pussegoda

MOORS FOR ME

What better than to bestride the moor
On spongy peat, feel the allure?
Observe wildlife delightful in their habitat;
Maybe see squirrel, stoat, mouse, vole or water rat.

Elements of wildness and mystery
With moving mists, untamed go free,
Engulf the unprepared, enveloping,
Disturbing and disorientating.

This is the environment that holds most appeal
To my whole self, so strongly I feel.
I'm grateful for sight and for mobility,
These gifts which enable me to move and see.

Ina J Harrington

THE BREAK OF DAY

An ascending mist enveloped the landscape,
Causing a mystical ambience of awareness,
Clouds were dark, and heavy, with appealing
Light struggling to appear.
As if by magic the hovering clouds parted,
Rays from the sun pierced the swirling mist.
Descending light amid the dewy grass
Appeared as pearls caressing each blade.
Highlighted by this magical dream, a chestnut
Stallion stood, embraced in the folds of mist,
Illuminated by the sun's rays, creating an awe-
Inspiring gift of nature.

Lorna Tippett

AUTUMNAL BLESSING

The year is on the wane.
Dusk comes early,
The nights now have a chill
That heralds cosy,
Fire-lit evenings,
The curtains drawn against
The wind and rain,
The sparkling frost.

But for the moment
I stand quietly
Out in my garden
Beneath the spreading branches
Of the great oak tree.
Softly they drop
Like feathers from
The grey-white doves,
They fall upon my head,
My shoulders,
The oak tree's leaves,
As though bestowing upon me
An autumnal blessing,
Reminding me that soon
All nature will embrace
Her winter sleep,
Renew her life
To blossom forth once more
When springtime comes.

Roma Davies

EXEMPLIFYING NATURE'S PARADISE

Where brambles and ivy cover the landscape, most intriguingly,
This, the lost gardens of paradise, with a haunting fragrant rose,
Where beautiful orange blossoms fall sedately, carpeting the floor,
Undisturbed by man, woman, or child, a carpet of pink and white
                                        petals slowly dies.

Only buzzing insects fly with fluorescent wings of light,
Where white mistletoe grows with bluebells of delight,
With undiscovered varieties that thrive in their millions,
Exotic coloured plants designed beautifully, shaped like wings.

By God's caring eye, and attention, consumed by design,
To the great palace of the earth, creatures live and die,
Where gorgeous water lilies abound, and below fish team unnoticed,
Where green willow hangs down above a stream of tadpoles and carp.

Buttercup and wild daisies, red poppies galore, with beautiful
                                        ladybirds in view,
With tall green cedar trees, oak, ash, and silver birch, that climb
                                        to the sky,
Sleeping like a surreal dream, in a bright land of love, and
                                        immeasurable beauty,
Where fairies cultivate and permeate their wonder, besides flying
                                        daddy long-legs.

Within the shadow of the trees, exemplifying nature's paradise,
Besides hill, valley, lake and stream, a waterfall cascades, dripping
                                        with silver droplets,
Where the bold eagle flies above the enchanted landscape, with a
                                        golden sun on the horizon,
The palette of a beautiful garden is displayed, over a mountain ridge
                                        of snow.

In nature's wood and forest, black beetle, earwig, worm and
                                        centipede forage,
Supreme nature is most evident with enchantment and surprise,
So palatial and inviting, where green moss and fern are prolific,
With fairy rings in abundance, with mushroom and toadstools, sky high.

Deer and stag dart by the ruined castle, overgrown by wild flowers,
Where a million dandelions float aimlessly below fluffy white clouds,
Clematis and primrose are magnificent, the smell so unique and divine,
Underneath the bluest skies of Heaven, after the rain comes a
                                        rainbow arc.

That stretches for miles through the blue-purple sky, and beyond,
With a myriad of colours, and blue tits, finch, sparrows and robins that
fly.

James Stephen Cameron

THE SAD SEA

The sad sea
sobbing to the shore.
The seagulls
crying and sobbing too.

The sea
throwing up her treasures
on the pretty shore.
The naughty, pinching crab
surging with the foam.
The rocks stab my feet
as I clamber to clear pools
reflecting turquoise.

'I will not cry,' says the sea
and heaves her waves instead,
flooding green and grey
to carve the coastline.

The gulls scream and swoop
to join the orchestra
and above, the stacking clouds.

Mary Braithwaite

THE TREASURE

The Earth, locked treasure chest,
dark and hard so long,
now spills its riches,
revealing golden aconites
collared in green,
close to the soil.
Nearby, the upright crocus
hooded in deeper gold,
followed by tall green stems
that promise daffodils!

Ruth Partington

ADONIA

Cutting her way through the deep blue sea,
splashes of blue-white foam spray heralding
her passage.
Further out, rays of sunlight reflect
as sparkling diamonds,
glittering as fireflies in the conflicting daylight.

The sea appears to vibrate.
It crashes and rolls. Wave after wave.
But where is it going; where has it been
and what does it carry with it? Apart
from Adonia, her passengers and crew.
Adonia knows her destination.

Nearby dolphins are demonstrating their
swimming skills and agility.
Gannets are swooping and diving nose-first
into the enticing sea and carrying off their prey.
The sun just continues to shine.
Its warm rays kissing soft flesh,
at times searing with its heat.

The sun sets. It disappears at a slow rate
on the horizon.
A glow. An ember.
Nothing.
There are no words to describe this sight.
I could weep, so beautiful it seems.
How I wish every day was a day spent
in the open, on the seas, with Adonia.

Naomi Donegan

HORIZONTAL IS THE NEW VERTICAL

Horizontal
is the new vertical -
an advertising notion
which makes no sense,
yet here is a tree,
its trunk horizontal,
branching to vertical,
in every other way
a normal tree,
it makes no sense,
it is only
an advertising notion,
yet reality rules,
it must be true;
if the advertisers
could see it
they would have to think
of something else
to surprise us,
grab our attention,
with a contradiction
which makes no sense.

Neville Davis

SUCH VIEWS

The sun sets slowly
from the moors
such views
are seldom seen,

While sitting by
the Ship Inn pub
on the banks
of the river Teign,

You won't believe
the way you feel
this sound just fills
your mind,

This piece of Devon
paradise
you know
you had to find.

James L Wood

SEASONS MOOD

Delights of spring -
Just a memory.
Hot summer sun
That scorched the earth
And dust of corn drying.
Perfuming the air -
Gone.
Autumn colours,
A sight so pure -
Contrasts
To skies of blue -
Have lifted
And sailed
Away.
And left?
The quietness
And tranquillity of nature's rest
In dormant harmony.
And the cold chill of air.
Life has gone,
But not forever,
As winter casts her spell
And turns the key to another year.

Lyn Sandford

THE FISHING BOATS

Insubstantial torrents
Misted in grey shrouds of pallid dawn;
Soft-row velvet fishing boats
Riding on the ocean way.
And the hard-edged rope
Burning the tired, barnacled fingers
No stranger to the deep, harsh spray,
As they wagered their wagging lines
Chugging their catch
To the harbour home:
With the stinking fish-head smells
Staring hollow-eyed
In their cruel death's embrace.

Yes, by the seagull's call
(Divided deum)
And stride-backed
Circling on the whiplashed wind
In Prussian blue and herdigo:
Harbouring sentinels
Of ever-change
To port and beyond.

Seen star-cast
By navigating charts,
Fluorescent pin-pricks
On God's giant ceiling:
Rainbow talked in whiskered mouth
Becalmed in oasis spared.
Yet pulled through on angel's wings
To the Guardian of the ocean Leviathan
With mountainous bounty
Force-fed in ritual sleep.
After, bleeding chaffed skin
On closed port-holes
Viewing the quantum foam.

There, a tip of shark's tail
On the sandy bottom floor.
Then a flash of gerry-light on Spithead,
As the roving adventurers
Return by the warrior's way
Froth-covered in horse-waves;
Spying land at last
With a cat's eye
Winked for one's girl
Waiting for their hearts
At the journey's end -
The only real love to die for.

Peter Corbett

AUGUST

The last long, hazy days of summer,
Dandelion clocks, spiders, spiralling on air
To be caught in small hands.
'One o'clock,' blow, 'two o'clock,'
Blow, 'three . . . '
The dog lies panting on the lawn,
Worn out from the sun's heat and
Chasing daddy-long-legs after dusk.
Smoke from my neighbour's barbecue
Fills my nostrils, mingling with
The smell of newly-mown grass.
August.

Joyce Walker

RAINBOWS

Rainbows are God's sunshine
Shining through the tears.
Breaking up the colours
To span across the years.
Sometimes storm clouds blow away
By God's almighty hand,
Letting out the sunlight
Drying up the tears.

Basking in the sunshine
Faith grows firm and strong
Breaking up resistance
If more storm clouds come along.
So rejoice in all the rainbows
Arching over all the fears.
Look for the sunlit pathway
To the land of no more tears.

Cecilia M Monk

OPEN YOUR EYES

Nature, God's gift of creation,
A gem in all its beauty.

Clods of earth frozen stiff,
Shuddering plants in the deadly cold.
Grassy banks, adorned with frost,
Glisten in their silver drapes.

A sense of anticipation,
Spring bursts forth, nature unfurls.
'Neath glossy laurels, snowdrops bloom,
Virgins of beauty, ice-cool white.

For courting blackbirds, it's bliss
In a gardener's paradise.
Leafy-decked trees, foliage so bright,
Blend in this magical scene.

Balmy, is the summer afternoon,
Perfumed lavender lingers in the air.
Roses, petals flushed pink and white,
Ramble in a Monet garden.

It's quiet now, time to reflect.
'Thanks for this wonderful world.'

Diana Frewin

BROADWATER AUTUMN

God has clothed the trees in autumn hues.
Some combine their summer green with gold
Some now greet the day in deepest red.
Cold winds move the silent lake and change
The algae carpet to clear, unsullied stream
Sun and clouds reflected there.

The earth is spread with fallen leaves,
Green grass joined with myriad shades
And on the lake, the wild birds glide,
Heron, swans with coot and hern,
Changing now to swift and sudden flight
While hungry pike make daring leaps.

God has moved the lake with gentle breeze
And blessed the water with his grace
Where sunbeams dance upon the stream
And autumn trees are mirrored there
With sun and cloud at water's edge,
Sign and pledge of God's beauty and His love.

Uvedale Tristram

EARLY SUMMER MORNING

The morning breaks open
like an egg
and I stand still
in its yellow warmth
before the day runs away
from my outstretched hands
as I try to catch it
to pin down its details
onto a crammed notice board
in the noisy kitchen.

But just for this moment
I can lean here
with eyes closed
face tilted upwards
to the shower of brightness
alone and quiet
part of the blue shadow
splashing the barn
sun-washed and dew-clean.

Helen Clarke

INSPIRED BY NATURE

I had always wondered what lay behind the dark green gate,
Beyond the high encompassing granite walls.
A secret world viewed only from above by passing birds
Inhabited by wild creatures great and small.
Today its secrets were revealed -
A quiet garden hewn from rocky hill
With vistas of the busy world beyond
And places just for being very still.
A garden made with love and vision
Where hard work reaps its own reward.
What joy to have created such a haven
A glimpse of paradise within this busy world.

D Harvey

RAVENSDALE

In Derbyshire's most secret heart,
Where wild colours burn into wild skies
Through the dark nets of trees
And distant suns blaze like neon baubles
Beyond the translucent window of night,
My youth, like a fragile egg,
Was pillowed by winds and grasses
Against the pillaging sins of man.

My heart beat with insects wings,
Pulsed with soft birdsong;
Longed to be impaled by peace -
To the beauty,
In this verdant cleft of suspended time,
Until earth is burnt in its own star's end
And a cool blanket of space
Swathes my soul in oblivion.

When my lips
Are sealed forever against my hungers,
When my loved one's cataclysmic tears
Fail to melt my mask of death:
Claim me Ravensdale,
Hold my spirit
In your pulsing power of peace,
My joyous womb of youth.

Dave Austin

NATURAL WONDERS

From time to time I conceive,
A blackbird searching in fallen leaves,
A butterfly flitting from flower to flower,
A cloud moving serenely overhead,
A mountain stretching into the stratosphere,
A robin splashing in a bird bath,
A star sparkling in the night sky,
A sycamore seed spinning slowly to the ground,
A waterfall cascading over the edge,
As the progeny of a poem.

Liam Heaney

To A Tree

Crimson beauty there you shone
All your leaves will soon be gone,
A sight so clear undefined
Of entire colours, vastness kind,
Yellows, reds, golden, green
Bringing nature's in-depth theme.

And then with one night of frost,
We see your beauty swept clean off,
Bringing your foliage pouring down
Revealing to us your valued mound
And then again you stand bare
Naked as an angelic glare.

Rest with restful dawn so pale
A mask of shallow symptoms term,
With winter's feelings, winter's cold
And a beautiful tree behold
As you show us your inner soul
Through our winter's existence.

Philip Robinson

DAWN

The English dawn brings dew in swirling white
That covers trees and lawns
Chorus by the vale are the shades of bluebells
Sending their perfume of a thousand morning voices,
Beside the flame vermilion of sky.

The sun is smiling on
The bonnie woodland green,
Fragrant with the beauty of the spring dawn,
The sparkling freshness, only morn can bring;
And overhead a canopy of blue
Fringes the skyline with golden hue.

The dawn brings a wonderful beginning,
A sliver of daylight, shifting skies bring dreamy chains
Blessed morning brings out birds singing.
This beauty is the happiest part of the day
Taking a wider view that shows the opening of the gates of freedom,
Having laughter and sunshine of love.

Heather Aspinall

EVOLUTION

Once mighty rocks
Above us they stood
Now crumbled and weather-beaten
Beneath our feet they are thrown

Tiny grains of sand
The shape of our foot
They do form
Yet they were the mountains
We could not climb

Now small and blown by the wind
They afford enjoyment to small
Living things
Like crabs and children with buckets and spades
Who happily stay all of the day

When they were alone up on that crag
Did they ever look at the sea
And even imagine
That one day
That shoreline they may be?

Angela Humphrey

A Morning Walk

As I walk across the field,
My horse comes eagerly to meet me,
Rivulets run down his hide,
Steam issues from nostrils quivering in the dampness,

The sun rises, proud and majestic,
Spilling light beams that reach across to the trees,
Casting long shadows deep into the forest,
I catch a glimpse of a deer, melting secretly into the thicket,

Mist rises ghostlike from the river valley,
Birds drift, lazily through the tendrils,
A lonely buzzard calls on high,
A ladybird below, struggles through the muddy ruts.

Dew sparkles on soft, damp moss
Hugging a fallen tree decorated with ivy and bindweed,
Dark, low clouds creep silently across the far horizon,
Threatening, glowering, heavy with rain,

A tiny wren bursts forth with glorious morning joy,
A blackbird rustles through the undergrowth,
Two partridges are nervously set to flight by the stealthy fox,
He pauses, listens, with one leg raised, sniffs the air,

As I turn back towards the track, I disturb a vole
That slips quickly and busily back into the hedgerow,
Blossom begins to glow in the soft, warm morning sunlight,
The gentlest of breezes whispering through the leaves,

My morning walk is almost at an end as I step out onto the lane,
I drink in the scents and sounds of nature as I turn for home,
Dazzled by the beauty which takes my breath away,
I eagerly await another stunning performance.

Teresa Prout

WINTER SUNRISE

Leafless tall trees merge into misty sky
With scarce a tremble in their long, dark twigs
In early morning greyness. Winter's here
And sluggish silence dominates the scene
With dreary emptiness.

I peer towards the east then I discern
A golden tracery trickling into view,
As gradually the darkened tree trunks take
An ebony look against the first faint rays
Of morning sun.

A saffron pattern strengthens and extends
On every side to sheen the polish on
The stately ash trees. I can even see
The topmost twigs now reaching for the sky
To seek the blue to come.

The golden eastern sun extends its power
Like some great fireball shouting to be seen
In all its glory. Dazzling the human eye
Resplendent in its will to dominate
The humble Earth.

Yet quickly as it came the colour fades
The shades of green and brown fan out once more
A bird call breaks the silence. Blue sky triumphs,
Though winter sunrise fades - it still stays in my mind
That brilliant sudden entrance of the dawn.
Day has come!

Margaret Connolly

FORESIGHT

Vibrant colour overhead
Yellow - orange - red.

From the bough leaves withered brown
already waft down
to lie in heaps under trees.
Squirrels run with ease
between rich colours that glow
and drab ones below
that crackle under our feet,
watch from their retreat.

Time to hide the nuts they find,
a hoard now in mind.
We pride ourselves on foresight -
squirrels also bright
who overcome present greed . . .
. . . winter food they'll need.
Autumn colour soon will go -
- this all squirrels know.

Vibrant colour overhead
Yellow - orange - red.

Chris Creedon

NATURE AT WORK

Take a route you have not been for some time,
You could be in for a brilliant surprise,
After a very hot summer,
With just enough rain to keep plants alive.

There are beautiful, bright autumnal colours to be seen,
Every shade of green has been put into the shade,
With the warm glow of burnished gold through to flaming red,
The countryside is alive with colour.

Here an unseen force with an uncanny power
Lifting the senses beyond imagination, is abroad,
There is a vibrancy superseding all else,
Taking you to impossible heights as onward you plod.

There is so much going on around us,
Take time to indulge in the spiritual renewal,
What better way to do this than
Reach for the hilltops, where gentle breezes blow.

There, away from the clutter and bustle
Of everyday living,
Reach for your inner peace,
A goal which cannot be surpassed.

Return to reality with a bump
And in your throat, let there not be a lump,
Feel regenerated, the cobwebs are gone,
Be now of good heart, rejoicing in song!

Time to get on with life once more,
Face up to that which is in store,
Know that each year brings its own revitalisation,
There is a light to lift our nation.

Away from wars of self destruction,
So let us take pleasure in what nature has to offer,
Be very much alive
And be very alert!

Mary Lawson

AUTUMN

Once my favourite season.
Landscapes petalled in red
and orange. I gathered
conkers, their smooth brown
circles cooled the palms
of blackberrying hands.

But now I spurn
shortening days, raincoat
evenings, the first frost.
Damp seeping to bone.
The calendar harvest
of absent birthdays.

Danielle Hope

THE AFTERMATH OF WINTER

Whichever way you look at it,
Life really is worthwhile.
Especially now at summertime,
It really makes me smile.
Now winter is behind me,
I am filled with our God's glory
As I see His new creation
Bursting forth to tell His story.
You know before I met my Saviour,
My eyes were closed and dim
But I notice everything now that Jesus has entered in.
Each tree and flower show God's love;
We all need His affection.
Like the plants, He nurtures us
Until we're brought to near perfection.
Like the caterpillar changes
From something crawling on the ground,
Into a graceful butterfly
Fluttering around.
That's how He will change me,
I will fall asleep one day
And waken, cradled in His arms
Encircled in His love, I pray.

Denise Seymour

THE PRIZE

As I sat waiting, I can't remember why,
I witnessed an argument beneath a bush.
A sparrow and a starling in a tug of war,
It involved much shove and pull and push.
The prize that they were striving for
Was a shiny cellophane strip.
They both hung on so tightly, but,
It was resistant and refused to rip.
Eventually the sparrow, spare and brown,
Not hampered by his obvious lack of size,
Won the tug of war, emerged the victor,
Fluttered off and upward with his prize.
The vanquished starling, still undaunted,
Not wishing to appear to be outdone,
Fossicked through the copious junk and litter
And found a strip just like the other one.
So both of them had finally been satisfied
And each could puff out his feathered chest,
As he proudly carried his cellophane window
Back to his mate and to their cosy nest.

Patricia Draper

THROUGH THE WOOD

I've trod this path many times before
From my old cottage on the moor.
Through the wood I wander on
It's been the same since time began.

Squirrels play amongst the trees
No other place I'd rather be.
It's early morning, haunting sounds
The beauty here, knows no bounds.

Through nature's canopy formed by trees
Shafts of sunlight start to squeeze.
Home to all the creatures here
I love this peaceful atmosphere.

Wild flowers grow at every turn
A splash of colour in the fern.
Songbirds sing their morning chorus
Such beauty here all around us.

A tiny shrew with feet so fast
Races through the dew-kissed grass.
A home-bound hedgehog creeps on by
Now tired after long, busy night.

So much I hear, so much to see
Just after dawn, the air is sweet.
Although I walk the same old path
I never tire, keep coming back.

Harry Murtagh

It's Raining Leaves

It's raining leaves.
Like manna from Heaven,
golden orbs from trees
lie in piles
of deep, multicoloured debris
stretching for miles.
Excited and noisy children
kick them high.
Swirling upwards
to the sky.
Trying to reunite them
with the trees
in the golden days
when it's raining leaves.

Maureen Reynolds

A SUMMER'S DAY

To walk down a leafy lane and see the sunlight bursting through the branches of the trees and hedges.

Throwing circles of light on the floor as if they were spotlights just put there to light your way.

Walking through the pools of light and then back into the shade, it takes a short time for your eyes to adjust again.

Just to stand in the shade and see the shafts of golden sunlight streaming through the lane canopy.

As the summer breezes rustle through the branches making the leaves dance and the branches to sway to and fro.

The pools of sunlight on the floor of the lane start to change shape, as if the edges were rippling.

Watching the squirrels dart back and forth across the lane in front of you, they stop briefly to look at you.

Then they're gone, off to the other side and up a tree, to peek from safety at you as you pass by.

Birds fluttering and calling as they hop from branch to branch in front of you, chasing flies through the shafts of sunlight.

Illuminated for a second or two before flying into the shade again, bees humming and butterflies sailing past on summer breezes.

As a feeling of tranquillity floods over you, then for the first time in your life you are one with nature.

Christopher Bean

A WALK IN THE PARK

The sun was shining,
A day to myself,
The park for a walk,
Out of the bushes,
Jumped two small
Children, they were hunting
For the bounty.

The cricket field empty,
The small train had gone,
Summer over, or
Was I wrong?
A sit on a bench,
The ducks a-quacking,
Flowers colourful,
I see the people,
Walking in the breeze,
Oh what a life,
One of ease,
I sat there quite
Amused, wouldn't you?

B Brown

INSPIRED BY NATURE

The spider makes her web,
Just like we make our home.
Ants go out to work every day,
Just like we do to make a living.
Lions eat the weak to survive,
Just like we eat meat to live.
Plants drink water to grown,
Just like we drink water to stop thirst.
Animals mate to keep their breed alive,
We mate to make generations.
Plants and animals need us to survive
And we need plants and animals to live.

Catrina Lawrence

LIFE

('Life may succeed against all the odds in moulding the Universe to its own purpose.' Freeman Dyson, conclusion to 'The Key To The Universe' by Nigel Calder, BBC 1977)

Jesting, we ask - what *is* life? Does that high
Mountain, towering above us, have it?
Perhaps not, yet the trees upon it do,
As does all of nature, happy, sullen,
Soft, or hard and full of wrath. When enters
Life into matter far and wide? The stars
Are alive with majesty and magic,
Galaxies strewn with generosity,
The Quarks abounding with the power of
The greatest intensity of the most
Concentrated thought and emotions deep.

Whence comes life? The Maker his secret keeps,
Until this lower life no longer sleeps
And life beyond life, calm, no longer weeps.

Desmond Tarrant

AUTUMN

Mother Nature is weaving her spells as she turns summer into
an autumn chill.
Bright green leaves turn into autumn gold,
Summer flowers fade and leaves blow down and cover the ground.

As I look out of my window on an autumn morn.
Spiders webs glisten like silver and pearl.
The sky is still blue, the sun is a fading yellow.
Low in the sky it sends out a shadow.

I look up and see flocks of birds flying high.
All heading south to escape the autumn sky.
So evening falls and the nights get darker,
Mother Nature carries on working her wonders.

Jenny Johnson

WHITMORE

Many years ago I glimpsed the lake
Shining through the hedge;
Now at last I've seen its beauty,
Walked around its edge.
How peaceful it all seemed!
No one else around . . .
When suddenly a squirrel
Scampered on the ground.
Then from the lake a heron rose,
Flew low across the ripples,
Put fear into the water hens
Where reed the surface stipples.
The darting swallows skimmed the mere
Where silver fishes shone
And from a seat I watched their play
As time dreamt slowly on.
Oh, what beauty! A dragonfly
Iridescent in red and green,
Hovered near with beating wings
Enhancing the Edenic scene.
How grateful I felt to find such peace
In a world torn by war and strife.
That glorious day will stay in my mind
To brighten the rest of my life!

E Balmain

SPRING-SPRUNG

Shake your winter wind-tossed hair,
free to these poignant make-it-so minutes
Close-cherishing these salient born-today verdances.
A garden surprised by rare April heat,
flirts new-budding, rain-questing, twig-tipped fingers
Skywards, upwards, high-heavening to the meddlesome birds
Who quit their pillage but to suffuse a fountainhead
water's diamond drops
Plumage-preening in new-moist rapture,
thus carelessly catching the mood of the moment.
Bold robins flaunt red-bibbed breast in temerarious threat
Towards songsters more feather-fluffed, pert-puffed than they
As medleys of magpies ape black and white waiters. Busy-so-busy
With a food-fussing, chirrup-chattering, dig-wriggling of worms
Whilst an ignorance of sparrows, hoi-polloi and odd-assorted,
impress the pageant by numbers alone
As do tadpoles by tens, tadpoles by thousands,
fecklessly frog-spawned in heedless tomorrows
Indifferent to nimble net-toting younglings with hungry jam jars, who
giggling gather this tail-twiddling harvest.
Fields by fields, fecundly yielding a leaping of lambs,
innocent ingenues milk-butting their mothers
Racing the rain in their joy-jumping youth,
charmingly heedless of foresight or future
And maybe, just maybe, a remarking of rainbow,
harlequin-hued in a mirage-mocked arc.
So salute to the spring with tributes of trumpets.
A new life, a new birth, nature fresh-hatched
Trailing know-nots but hope-fors, the secret tomorrows,
all cross-carried in its wave-pleated wake.

Sarah Blackmore

BIRDSONG

Amid flurries of feathers
The birds rejoice
In founds of song -
Celebrations of sound

Plumes wheel
And comet around
From out of a golden egg in the sky

Music fills
The blue air
Arcs in a rainbow
Of crystallised joy.

Vanessa Burgar

SOLITUDE

('No man is an island of itself, every man is a piece of the continent, a part of the main' - John Donne (Devotions upon Emergent Occasions and Several Steps in my sickness)

The city. Where solitude is
An unenviable friend, to so many
Unenviable people.

As I sit on a weather-beaten bench,
Dedicated to some nobody -
My representative in a bygone era -
I listen to the silence;
A muted land across the ocean
That separates me and mine.

But car and man surround me.
To them I am but a spectre -
A translucent shape, at which they stare,
Yet never observe.
To me they matter not,
For this island is mine alone.

For an eternity I can be alone,
Unharassed by the familiar,
Acutely aware of my atoll,
Of my conscience.

Here I feel at home,
Amid a thousand shades of grey.
Here I can be me, content living,
Yet existing to no one but myself,
Heeding nought but the breeze of my mind.

Dave Savage (18)

A Wonder Sea Beach

The silent sea beach apparently undisturbed,
Shortly becomes crowded with sailors,
Tradesmen, labours - all appearing
Busy, care-worn and full of tensions!
They are looking forward
To cargo-laden ships,
To be unloaded, anchoring near the shore;
Now the sinking red sun,
Big and mild, throws golden
Yellow beams from the extreme west horizon
And fills everything with a soft grandeur
Across the waves and the beach!
It's a cool September afternoon,
Several grey-white sea birds
Would be seen coming from unknown
Places and perching on high points of ships,
Or, on a large tree beside
The foggy, shadowy forest deep!
Soon the last glimmers of the soft sun
Falling on the birds make them
Significant by their grey mantles
And bright bills glowing so mysterious
In the fineness of beauty of the departing beams!
The evening shadows gradually enclose
Everything on the beach quietening
And a haunting darkness tends to descend
All upon the deep sea swaying;
Ships like lighted black bodies
Move out as threatening rovers
And the sea birds in their silent flights
Make strange swinging motions
Of dark wings like the low rhythmic waves;

Unknown to them are the dins of dusty cities,
They are peace incarnate like
The infinity of stars shining
So magnificent in the Heavens vast!

Kalyan Ray

GIFT OF DOLPHINS

Dolphins grace our world you know.
To show us how to heal and grow.
They touch our souls with their grace.
They are here to help the human race.
Their love is tender and lasts forever.
Patience they have is never ending.
So when they touch your soul
You know what love is
For that is their goal.

Rose Mills

BRACKEN

The herald of tree-turning
Is the bracken, bronzed
In the sunlight, like an attic shield,
Harbinger of autumn.

Trees turn slowly,
Yet suddenly have arrived
In flame-gold, flame-orange, flame-red -
Still, utterly still,
Poised,
Waiting in glory
For the unseen forces to come
And wrestle with the fragile hold
That breaks and lays their glory
At our feet -
To be scuffed along,
Trampled through
And trod with plodding pleasure
By kids and grown up children.

The bracken stays,
Yielding its depths of sunlit bronze
Gradually
To the muted tones of winter.
It, too, has its glory in the fall.

Rosemary Wells

THE NASTURTIUMS

Working in the garden
    I find seeds I sowed
        the day before you died.

So this is how much life
    there has been since you.

    Three weeks
        three inches
            and three green leaves.

Julia Wheeler

LAURA

She froze a hyacinth
and let it flower forever in the freezer.
The petals stayed firm and blue,
plump with frost, the sweet intact.

She was winterless, a child of spring,
her beginnings vague, her endings unimaginable,
patched up with plasters and wrists like twigs
with old scars whitening into bangles.

The bracelets ball and chained her to her girlhood,
along with all the other wounds
without a scare - more sting than salt -
that brand the soul like butter and don't heal.

The flower of her girlhood froze -
summer trapped forever in the freezer.
And what of those who froze her -
will they pay the price and recognise.

The winter in her eyes?
Outside the hyacinths are short on spring -
root deep in rain.

Karen McKoy

COLOURS OF MORNING

It's a perfect art - a morning-lit sky;
A flame set against a backdrop of blue,
Where, in the quiet glow, verdant hills stand,
And notes of birds fill a pink solitude,
Where an airy gold web holds deepest thought,
Everything reflected in lambent hues -
The halcyon colours spanning the ken,
All melding into the day's pulchritude.

Donna Ryan

RIPPLES OF CRYSTAL WATER

Ripples
on the blue water
are like diamonds
captured in the light
as I swim to try and hold them
they disappear in my hand
and yet they are sparkling everywhere
white bright
pure as light
shimmering and shining
amongst the shifting surface
of the clear crystal water
where the blue water
ripples.

Gilly Jones-Croft

PEACE IN THE GARDEN

She is busy with dust and suds
He with toil and soil
But in the balm of a summer evening
In the glow of the setting sun
They rest and sip warm coffee
And the peace of the garden is theirs.

Her thoughts are with the children
His are with problems to solve
Midst hard won lawn and flowerbeds
Surrounded by colour and space
They sit in comfortable silence
And the peace in the garden is theirs.

She ponders how it will be
He plans for what is to come
They walk life's path together
Summers and winters alike
And through all of its varying seasons
The peace of the garden is theirs.

Margaret J Wallace

MY GARDEN

Now I'm retired with hours to spare
It's time to use my gardening flair
Pruning the roses and cutting the grass
What are you doing, my neighbours ask?
I'm fifty-nine now and raring to go
When will I get that marvellous show?
The roses are blooming, the hanging baskets look fine
The grass will get greener in a matter of time
The work is endless can't you see
My dear wife will throttle me
She doesn't see me very much
I'm up in the garden, no time for lunch.
The greenhouse looks a proper mess
That's what I'll have to be sorting out next
I want my tomatoes to grow to the eaves
Blimey, that will be a bit of a squeeze.
I must go now my wife's calling me,
'Come on it, it's time for your tea.'

D Jones

BORN FROM A SEED

Born from a seed,
Given time to grow
It blossoms,
Time passes
And the beautiful flower
Withers and
Dies.

Marc Robinson

DAZZLING DISPLAYS

Large baskets, packed with flowers, hang from hooks,
Greeting each new visitor that arrives
With dazzling arrays of rainbow colours.
Red fuschias hang down majestically,
Prima ballerinas of basket world.
Dark blue lobelia weaves its way through,
Sneaking over the edge for better views.
Petunias peep out round foliage,
Their violet and indigo flowers
Frame orange and yellow marigold blooms.
Can you count the myriad shades of green?
From small beginnings, planted in late spring,
The baskets, hanging in all their glory,
Announce to the world that summer is here.

Angela Pritchard

WHY ARE THEY NOT LISTENING?

Hey little sparrow
Sitting high up in the tree
Have you got a song to sing
Especially for me
I love to hear you singing out
Your chirpy little song
It puts a spring in my step
As I'm wandering along
Many people pass by
Totally unaware
They do not hear you singing
They're not conscious you are there
The world is far too busy
To listen to you sing
But if they did they'd realise
Just what joy that you can bring.

Karen Hodgetts

OCTOBER MORN

It's an October morn and the dawn ascends,
The sparkle of the dew on the grass,
Creates a hue that no artist can comprehend.
The calling of the ducks
As they wing their way
To feed upon the stubble, in fields not too far away.
Begins as a single call,
That builds into a cry so loud,
That it becomes a solid sound.
The freshness of the breeze is so invigorating,
It gives you a boost to go on walking
And listen to nature talking
Whilst looking with eyes wide open,
Can be refreshing, without a word being spoken.
You sit a while contemplating
Whilst nature becomes so illuminating.

Toby

OCTOBER'S WAIT

October is
The month
For dying.
Trees understand
October's demands;
They change in
Reticent obedience
To nature's way.
The hard part
Is the wait
For finality.

Alice Parris

SEASCAPE

A soothing hum belies,
the imminent danger.
Slowly, it gains momentum,
surging forward,
sure of winning.
A menacing cloak,
of arrogant mischief,
enveloping all in its path.

A waspish hissing joins,
the swelling tempo.
Transformation now complete.
Vicious currents lash
out with venom.
Squalls of spray,
add random spite.
Hisses convert to howls.

Briefly it subsides,
pausing for respite,
sneering ominously,
at a cowering sea wall.
Then swiftly relaunches,
battering blindly,
pouring its salt into
open wounds.

Finally it recedes,
replete from exertion,
backtracking through
trails of destruction.
Marshalling resources,
for its next encounter.

Paul Kelly

ON THE DEFORESTATION OF AMERINDIAN LANDS BY VENEZUELAN RANCHERS

Today such men will soon undo
The age of nature's art,
A time when only jungle grew
And hushabye'd a chosen few -
A people set apart.
The tractor's roar,
The buzz saw's screaming whine
Tear out what went before
The age of Earth's decline.

What once was wild is tamed to field
Enclosed by barbed wire fence.
The virgin ground is raped to yield
A harvest boom so they can shield
Their egoist pretence.
Such hunt the free!
In progress drunk they cannot wait
Till every man's a refugee
From Nature's balanced state.

Gardiner M Weir

NATURE'S BOUNTY

The wonder of nature,
Rich bounty of life,
Magnificent coloured flowers,
The marvels of ocean life.

What jewels of vivid beauty,
The wild, tropical birds,
The diversity of all animals,
A myriad of life.

C E Atkinson

NATURE'S JOURNEY

The seasons
Marked by trees
Our time is told
No clocks, or calendar
Unfold
To tell us all we need.
Bare boughs
Uplifted to the skies
The winter wild
Proclaims
And gentle buds of green
Each spring is named.
Bright sun
Through shimmering leaves
Casts dappled light
Into the room
Warm summer's lease alas
Is gone too soon.
The fall
With autumn winds
Disturbs a shower of gold
And scatters streets
And gardens
In the rain and cold.
The seasons
Marked by trees
Our time is told.

Marion P Webb

AUTUMN'S GOLD

Yellow, orange, red and brown the colour of the leaves
Autumn is upon us, we know this by the trees
The forest is a blaze of colour, a beautiful sight to see
Squirrels very busy, jumping from tree to tree
They're busy gathering acorns, as many as they can hold
Storing them for winter, when the days are cold.

The smell of wet, damp leaves bring memories back to me
Running through falling leaves when I was young and free
Knocking conkers off the tree requires quite a skill
Our great grandfathers played this game, I guess kids always will
Bright, shining conkers on long pieces of string
If you can break mine off, you'll be sure to win.

Brenda Bartlett

WINTER HELIOS

Under the cloak of a winter's sky
skeletal trees cowered against the
buffeting of punching storms
that threw chaffinches into the air
frightened and unfed
lichen-coated willow, shed fingers to lie
dead in the moist, heavy grass
forced flat by ever dripping skies
yet within this grey, heavy scene
sits the hinting white ghost of a snowdrop
winter's own helios.

Neal Moss

STORM

Rain, sluicing the cliff face,
Varnishes with wetness rusts, golds, greens and granite greys
In that primordial crag; wind, scything the headland,
Chops furious waves in the tumultuous seas.

Blind, boundless space and endless time.

Here, ears thick with noise, sheltered from turmoil
In this hollowed cleft, he watches with insane delight
Pale, wind-sped clouds stream leaden skies
Slashed, suddenly, with rents of sharpest blue.

And everywhere the smell of stones and water.

Such threatening, such fearsome turbulence
Menaces and terrifies, astounds, exhilarates,
Such fiercely thrilling savagery overwhelms
And saturates the marrow of his bones.

What elemental force of waves and wind strives here -
How very small he seems . . . and vulnerable . . .

Gillian Howarth

MOODY OCEAN PLANET BLUE

Moody ocean planet blue,
I love you.

Sometimes you are ill,
Cough and spurt a volcanic hill.
Hot larva,
Burning red,
You become so angry,
Toss in your bleeding bed.

But moody ocean planet blue,
I love you.

With your sumptuous scenery,
Sometimes dangerous, but divine,
Only spoiled by,
Some of man's ugly building skyline.

Mother of nature,
Father of soul,
With enduring life,
You keep control.

You breathe a soothing sigh,
Calm your hurricane,
All is peaceful,
All is tame.

Then you whip the waves again,
You're upset and you moan,
But you are,
My bounteous, beautiful home.

Moody ocean planet blue,
I love you.

Then hush, hush!
You offer no rush,
As your sensuous breezes,
Gently brush,
My thankful face,
As you travel in space,
A living suitcase.
And, I go happily in love with you,
My moody ocean planet blue.

Carol Ann Darling

COULD ALL THIS BE YESTERDAY

The majestic willow tree,
Her trunk embedded with dark wavy grooves of time.
Thick bark with moss-green growth.

Silvery green leaves,
Sway in the breeze.
She splays her branches high,
Makes a passage way underneath.

Her weeping leaves, like silver green ribbons,
Touch my greying head of hair.
The majestic willow tree,
From heavy drops of rain she covered me.
Soft, fine yellow branches
Fell like strands of embroidery threads.

Watching her grace a hollow passageway,
Ashen leafy ribbons, move all curly.
Her branches sway protecting overhead.
Making me feel,
Just like a princess of greenery.
This fine willow tree, she sparked a curiosity.

A smile came as I reached out my hand,
Coyly she reached the leaves on high,
Of another of her born species,
Intermingling a silvery green glow,
Against a sky of cloudy grey,
I, in all this finery!

The passageway of wonderment, lead to a motorway,
With busy cars toing and froing and I am glad that I am slow today.
That I cannot drive the cars of the motorways.

Maria Ann Cahill

MOOD INDIGO

While following a path across Knox Hill,
I leaned against a fence one autumn day,
To pause awhile and view the distant scene
Where sea and skyline met in harmony.
A horizontal cloud hung lazily,
Translucent in an amber velvet glow.
Between it and the surface of the sea,
A tawny trail of smoke pursued its course
Across a satin sky of palest green.
A rainy sun surveyed the furrowed fields
Below the hillocks that surrounded me.
I lingered, loath to shatter such tranquillity,
When suddenly, the shrill cry of a seagull startled me.
I shivered. Time to go. I must move on.

Kathleen McGowan

AUTUMN

The days are shorter now, though oh so lovely.
The nights draw in and we can settle round the fire.
We continue our interests; reading, writing,
Music, craftwork - to name but four.

We watch more television than in summer.
Whilst outside nature takes its course.
The leaves are turning a beautiful golden brown; and russet red,
Birds begin to migrate to warmer climes;
A squirrel scampers on the wall, taking nuts to his nest.

The leaves begin to fall,
Horse chestnuts fall into the lane,
Flowers in the garden begin to wilt,
Rowan berries and rose hips begin to show.
Pussycat curls up around the fire.

Yet this is an Indian summer,
The sun shines, oh so brightly in the day.
The last days of summer now behind us.
The sun will soon bid rest to nature once again.
Yet nature will take its course and lead us on - to another year.

Janet Cavill

MELODY LANE

The trees moved in step with me, trudging through mud and sludge,
an army singing.
Deep bases, mossy green cloaks skirting trunks, broad beamed
contraltos, silver-leafed tenors, little high-pitched sopranos.

Creaking boat songs echoed round the valley.
Birds whirled and whistled dancing with the moving branches.
Happy winds joined in my favourite song
Notes and scales creating new rhythms.

The 'Choral Society' of 'Melody Lane' was in full swing,
No dress rehearsal, the colours dazzling
as the sun came out like a spotlight.
I stopped in my tracks, the trees were still and watching,
Like a painting, a game of musical chairs.
Time to move on, I can face the music.

Maura Malone

NATURE'S JOY

To walk in quite peaceful solitude,
To feel the gentle breeze upon my face,
The breeze that dances high in trees with haste,
The smell of honeysuckle, hops now brewed,
To rest on nature's bed of grassy folds,
The bleating lambs, the sun that warms my soul,
The birds who flock to feed on furrowed soil
And sky so blue, the fields of corn now gold,
The horses galloping so free and wild,
With buzzards floating gently, thermal air,
Along the slopes of purple heather fair
And distant squares of blue and yellow fields,
The hills seen rising above the plain,
So beautiful in their design and reign.

David M Walford

MARCH SONG

The March song kisses mountain walls,
Canyons of breathing echoes,
Recording in their resumes
My whispered dialogue of farewells.

Farewells embodying reluctance,
The reluctance of renewed warfare,
Of the losing and fighting and winning,
But mostly of the losing, the dour forsaking.

A song of an ancient bronze god,
Cracked and coloured earthen ochre,
Sinewy legs planting shadows in the spring fields,
Muscled chest scarred with bloodied iron ribs.

A song of a virgin's ambivalent regret,
Regret of surrender, of haemorrhaging sex into soil,
First love freely given, like the vestal Rhea Silvia,
To some sporadic god of death.

And a song that so clearly defines
My prayers for a future life,
Of love and peace avenged of neglect,
So reborn, reclaiming a better world.

Tony Bush

SUMMER EVE

Beneath a mackerel sky aglow
With golden light, as sun prepares
To take its leave at end of day,
From high aloft the swirling swifts
In weaving dance, as skates on ice,
Are still pursuing hidden prey.
They seemingly survey our slow
And restless dodgem-car attempts
To move amongst the crowds of those
At summer fair below, where noise
And rowdy music clash with shouts
Of glee from roundabout and hum
Of diesel engine's steady throb.
But few discern those silent birds
Whose gliding forms, at ease in air
As fish in ocean's deep, now seem
A gentle blessing sent to keep
A watch on those of us below
Who wonder why we're not content
To live out lives in harmony;
Without the need for constant ploys
To lift our sense of pointless toil.
They'd give our random moves a grace
To match the rhythms they display.
But, as clouds acquire a tinge
Of red, those wheeling shapes depart
To leave a sense of emptiness;
But also praise for such as them
Who lead their lives without the aid
Of manufactured thrills and hopes.

Henry Disney

CHANGING TIMES

Autumn leaves lie forlorn up on the ground.
While they adorned the trees from whence they came,
Their autumn colours of rust, orange and gold,
Brought so much pleasure and warmth,
To those who gazed upon their final moments.
When they have fallen and are dry, they still bring pleasure.

On a cold winter's morning we tread or scoot our way through
the leaves,
They make a sound like biscuits being crushed,
Causing us to think of family and friends,
Reminding us of the past year, of days gone by and log fires.
So much chattering and laughter - so much joy and suffering.
From something as simple as fallen leaves.

When those fallen leaves become wet.
They are like gruel, sticky and slippery to walk on.
They then remind us of a Victorian workhouse.
Bleak and uninviting and dangerous to be in.
Autumn is a twin-edged sword,
It comes and it goes, bringing pleasure and distress.

I R Matthews

SUMMER HAS GONE

Summer has gone
And with it the warmth and comfort to stop and look
At clouds that float by at an intentionally slow pace
While you search for a similar shade of blue in your memory.

Autumn bites playfully
Prompting trees to sigh in shades of brown
And let the winds shake these troubles from their boughs
As energies are drawn inwards for the coming freeze.

Winter and spring await
The whites and silvers held in store
And the colours to follow freshly buried in the ground
Are only ideas of some future landscape.

Doug Cairns

NATURE

This world is such a lovely place, the sun rising in the sky at morn,
another day with golden dawn
Azure blue in summer sky, fluffy like clouds drifting by
Trees with cherry blossoms, pink and white,
their perfume brings us sheer delight
Purple heather covering hills, trumpets of the daffodils
Different seasons throughout the year, myriads of colour everywhere
The luscious grasses with shades of green,
trees in autumn shedding leaves
River gushing towards the sea, stormy weather changing scene
Salmon rising to the flow, hankering after the sea they go
Every day a different view, see the rainbow spectrum too,
spectacular in its different hues, purple, red, orange and blue
How lucky we are; in this world of ours,
so much variety in our flowers
Imagine a world of black and white,
no stars to shine in the darkest night
Treasure this beauty from day to day;
colours can chase the blues away.
Walk in the country, climb up a hill,
look down below and see a patchwork quilt.

Joan Prentice

An Early Observation

i watched a friend spend time with God today
first thing after waking up this morning
he stretched, yawned, rolled over a bit
(scratched himself a few times)
and immediately
walked right past me
(without so much as a word)
and kneeled in front of a glory-filled bay window
and talked to God
his Creator
his Master
his Best Friend
it was only for a few moments
so there was no time for an 8 point sermon
on the predestination (or lack there) of the elect
to be imparted
but there was more than enough time
for the love to flow
afterwards he did greet me
by ambling over
and putting his head in my hand

i'm writing this while rubbing his belly
as he lays curled up on the floor beneath me
and i can't help but think of
the things that you can learn
from a dog.

Matthew E Henry

LOST

I watch the figure walk away, ever smaller,
now as untouchable as the very sun
which blazes down on this September Sunday.
I am numb as I study the scene before me:
shirt-sleeved men, women in summer finery
squint whilst departing the cool, dark church
as a woman in wheelchair peruses the park
perhaps never to feel such glorious weather again
for we are free from the stifling August heat
and a refreshing breeze rustles yellowing trees,
golden leaves clinging to their roots
like cubs to the safety of a mother.

Church bells and birdsong are the serene sounds
and the felicitous tone of children's laughter
as butterflies flicker across a deep, azure sky.
The figure has now disappeared from view
yet children still play and the sun still shines.
It's a day to savour, taking pleasure in being alive
but I wish for black skies and rain to arrive.
The lake sparkles as if bedecked with jewels
and it's as if I've let slip a priceless diamond
into the water of the most fathomless sea,
what I've lost will never return to me.

Guy Fletcher

THE BEGONIAS

The begonias held the livelong day
In beauteous profusion colourful, gay;
Concave sepals, yellow, red and blue,
Cradled by the sun, offered no scent, that's true.
But in bushy brilliance growing there
Hardy, to withstand September's cooler air.
With those tiny, yellow centres too -
Giving minuscule magic for me to view;
And with every single glance I took,
They seemed to present an almost waxen look.
Their touch was silky surprisingly,
Yet so enchanting in its delicacy.
The summer's gone now and autumn's here,
Unhindered, winter is fast approaching, near.

Alexander Winter

MOTH-LIGHT

Her moth-flight is an exploration tortuous
Of the deepest, darkest, secret places.
Shaman wings reach out into
Caverns and shrines of deep mining networks
Where the pious and virtuous
Are stacked and hoarded.

What price now their sophistry and verity?

Her moth-sight
Blindly burrowing and tunnelling,
Delving and ferreting
Through black-ink spaces,
Set in windless and sunless places.

Relentlessly encrypting pathways
Between gothic buttresses . . .
(Chased with passion)
Below legendary monuments . . .
(Wrought and encrusted with the sweat of men).
Here generations traded histories for futures.

Now in the employ of frenzy,
(Aegis came from no quarter)
A single candle flame emerges
And her moth-life is extinguished.

Above, a retinue of pale angels
Standing sentinel, bear silent witness to the
Convergence of the whole of her life,
To this one flare-point . . . The moth-flare.

And so a million miracles disappeared in moth-light.

Robert Vizard

WINDOWPANE

As the rushing wind goes passing by
The falling leaves come floating down
Now that autumn is here
The wind and rain are here to stay
Pitter-patter, pitter-patter goes the rain
As it runs down our windowpane
Now all is wet and shining bright
Soon the sun will come out
And dry our windowpanes.

Ella Wright

RAIN

There are those who give with joy and that joy is their reward.
For life goes not backward nor tarries with yesterday.
And together we shall rejoice through all the seasons.
Build a house with affection and care.
'Joy is greater than sorrow.'
Have you peace, have you beauty
The breath of life is in the sunlight
When your spirit goes wandering upon the wind
Stand in the sunlight with your back to the sun
Who commands the skylark not to sing
When you sit in the cool shade of the trees
And share the peace and serenity of the distant fields.
When the storm comes with the mighty wind, thunder and lightning.
It is the pleasure of the bee to gather honey from a flower
But the flower's pleasure is to give honey to the bee.
For the bee, the flower is its fountain of life.
Beauty is kind and gentle
A man needs change, but not his love or desire
The mist that drifts away at dawn
Leaving any dew on the ground in the fields
Through it rises and becomes cloud
It falls down as rain.

Beaney Hall-Quibell

NATURAL REMEDY

Sunflower,
towering high.
As autumn dews approach,
your golden petals radiate warmth
and joy.

Diane Bowen

FROM A ROSE GARDEN

Birdsong sprinkles stillness
Touching gently vast vibrations of calm.
Leaves litter ground, autumnal trees
Tower skyward, symbols of living peace.
Now, your nearness, from beyond
Groping utterance light beyond light
Comes space, time, you dear Mum
Free indeed in eternity, far from
All the pain and, love never dies
Love is living and binding here
In rose-flowered peace, here in nature
There is rest and peace at last.

George Coombs

THE WORLD IN THE RAIN

The world is one scared woman in the rain.
Across the cups of silver she runs
To find a house, any house where her laugh
Will build a fire, where in some tiny place
The sun's old fiddle plays a song.

Marion Schoeberlein

PROGRESS WHAT OF IT?

A 300 year old oak is subsequently felled
this gives way to a sea of concrete.
Dual carriageways and the aptly numbered motorways -
supplying society the so-called life blood of a floundering
material-driven industrialised world.
The concrete veins that so ruthlessly cut swathe through the
patchwork green and yellow fields, so what of the hedgerows
                                            of yesteryear?
The streaming HGVs carrying their loads, a resemblance of platelets,
a service to the industries that thrive upon this, this obnoxious, choking
swathe of man's progress - the ticking by to the hour of the
                                            doomsday clock.
The fate of man lost in the nuclear and chemical abyss!
The ruination of the present and the future and flogging
Nature to death, this is society's all-spreading, consuming,
                                            malignant, cancer.
The lifeblood of a civilised, progressive global economy.
For the masters of this world are we?

Jonathan Covington

DAYS ASTIR

A crisp morning awakening
Breathless cloudless mood
Geese and mallards fly in formation

Rural winter space
Secrets drifting freer
Grassy-coloured marshland

Bedraggled tracks calling
Beautiful landscapes unearthed
Seeking no warning

Creaky chilled misdeed
Bruised sentimental places
Senseless clinical amnesia

Vaporised mortal life
Isolated nightingale sounding
Souls of sunset laughter.

Sharron Hollingsworth

THE WINTER IS NOW COME

And the bitter cold shivers on our backs,
The days are short and dark.
We have left the best summer behind.
The people suffer the longer it stays cold,
There is no more sun to shine.
We have to endure the longer cold by day and night
Until the spring will bring the lovely sun to warm our cold backs.
Until then life for all of us is a hell.
I for one hate the cold, but gloomy days are here to stay.
We must do our best to keep warm and not catch any colds
Until the hot summer comes back to all of us.
Be cheerful, do not go down, keep your moral.
I do understand the winter is bad for everyone.
We cannot go out to walk in the sunshine in the green parks
                                    and the lovely countryside;
But we must do our best to keep cheerful until the summer
                                                is back again.
Long live the sun and the green valleys of England!

Antonio Martorelli

THE KITCHEN TREE

Given to me for my fiftieth birthday
It lives in my kitchen
A cupressus tree
Maybe it will have a life outside one day
Perhaps it will really grow then
My cupressus tree

But I like it to remind me of a kind thought
A gift from a special friend
This cupressus tree
My mother had just died when it was bought
Serving to remind me there is no end
When your mind is free

To plant it in the garden means it could be lost
If I ever have to move away
Leaving behind my kitchen tree
Giving it room to grow could have a cost
The risk of losing it holds sway
I want to keep my cupressus tree.

George Raymond May

NEVER MISS THE RAINBOW

The rain came like a blessing,
From the glorious skies of Heaven.
And it poured and poured,
Tears of simple joy, crystal clear beads
The earth soaked it in, thirstily.
And I the rich girl, with a beautiful house,
Born to riches and spoiled with luxury,
I ran out and danced in the rain;
Free at last . . . from a promising future,
That I could only see as a demon.
And then, when the rain let up,
I felt the nip in the air, tingling my neck,
And creeping down my spine.
I shared a quiet moment with the sweet man
A man with no ambition and no desires.
We gazed above as a rainbow smiled at us
I looked on at the colours, as he whispered,
'Walk on my child and climb on high,
But never miss the rainbow in the sky.'

Nicole Braganza

YOU AIN'T HAVING HIM FOR YOUR DINNER

There's a robin
Just landed on a tree
Feeding on bread
Given by an old lady
She watches
From the kitchen window
Frightened not to scare
Heads for the door on tiptoe

She stands in the garden
Next to a chair
Silently mesmerised
She smiles
Cos she cares
The robin
Lets out a cry
The old lady smiles
He has just said to her, 'Hi.'

Then a squirrel
Climbs over the fence
Looking a bit frightened
Seeming a bit tense
It looks around
And watches the bird
Busy eating bread
Doesn't seem to be scared

But then a cat
Put an end to all that
Jumps from behind the dustbin
A split second to sin
It missed
The squirrel by a whisper
The old lady calls,
'You ain't having him for your dinner.'

The cat
Looked around to see that
The squirrel headed for the tree
Next to the robin he shares a seat
Both of them
Looking on down
As the cat lets out a purr
And thinks to itself
When and how?

Will he get his treat
As he sits next to the old lady's feet?
She calls out his name angrily,
'Thomas!' in vain.
The cat let out a miaow
And straight away it cowers on down
And slowly walks into the house
Just like a frightened mouse.

The old lady
Gives out a sigh,
A sigh of relief.
The squirrel knows why
She takes from her apron
Some monkey nuts
Throws them towards the smiling creature
Some titbits and bits of fluff.
The cat
Looks from the kitchen window
The old lady points to him and shouts,
'Thomas no! No!'
She won
No damage was done
The cat got some milk
The old lady an iced bun.

Stephen A Owen

LIVING IN THE COUNTRY

I used to live in the country.
I remember the grouse flying sharply,
calling, 'Go back, go back!'
The red deer running with their antlered stags.
The heather which blooms in August.
Nearer the house, below the hill,
the blue tits, coal tits, great tits
and sometimes crested tits
called squeakily while feeding
in the dense trees.

Rabbits used to come into the garden,
but cats keep them away now.

An otter, an eel, a pike,
in the small loch.

Salmon and trout in the Spey
I once fished.

The autumn fruits, both wild,
and from the garden.
Our plums were always delicious.

The capercaillie - the wild turkey -
was glimpsed occasionally in the pine woods.
The black cock appeared among the rocky hills
as did the roe deer in the nearby birch wood;
also woodcock.

Whooper swans and geese in the winter,
on the cold fields. The water rat plops
into the nearby stream.

You can guess this is the
Scottish Highlands. We have wild cats
and pine martens.
Nowadays there is a zoo
with wolves, bison and tame eagles.
The osprey fishes for salmon
in the lochs with his talons.
Various owls are there too.

Waders abound in the marshy valley -
curlew, sandpiper and the snipe drums.
There used to be corncrakes, but they've
disappeared with intense farming.
Woodpeckers come occasionally.

Finally, I still can taste
the home-grown vegetables from my visits.

Keith Murdoch